MW01155947

ALYSSA MILANO

A Real-Life Reader Biography

John Bankston

Mitchell Lane Publishers, Inc.
P.O. Box 619 • Bear, Delaware 19701

Mitchell Lane PUBLISHERS

Second Printing

Real-Life Reader Biographies

Paula Abdul	Christina Aguilera	Marc Anthony	Lance Armstrong
Drew Barrymore	Jan & Stan Berenstain	Tony Blair	Brandy
Garth Brooks	Kobe Bryant	Sandra Bullock	Mariah Carey
Aaron Carter	Cesar Chavez	Roberto Clemente	Christopher Paul Curtis
Roald Dahl	Oscar De La Hoya	Trent Dimas	Celine Dion
Sheila E.	Gloria Estefan	Mary Joe Fernandez	Michael J. Fox
Andres Galarraga	Sarah Michelle Gellar	Jeff Gordon	Mia Hamm
Melissa Joan Hart	Salma Hayek	Jennifer Love Hewitt	Faith Hill
Hollywood Hogan	Katie Holmes	Enrique Iglesias	Allen Iverson
Janet Jackson	Derek Jeter	Steve Jobs	Michelle Kwan
Bruce Lee	Jennifer Lopez	Cheech Marin	Ricky Martin
Mark McGwire	**Alyssa Milano**	Mandy Moore	Chuck Norris
Tommy Nuñez	Rosie O'Donnell	Mary-Kate and Ashley Olsen	Rafael Palmeiro
Gary Paulsen	Colin Powell	Freddie Prinze, Jr.	Condoleezza Rice
Julia Roberts	Robert Rodriguez	J.K. Rowling	Keri Russell
Winona Ryder	Cristina Saralegui	Charles Schulz	Arnold Schwarzenegger
Selena	Maurice Sendak	Dr. Seuss	Shakira
Alicia Silverstone	Jessica Simpson	Sinbad	Jimmy Smits
Sammy Sosa	Britney Spears	Julia Stiles	Ben Stiller
Sheryl Swoopes	Shania Twain	Liv Tyler	Robin Williams
Vanessa Williams	Venus Williams	Tiger Woods	

Library of Congress Cataloging-in-Publication Data
Bankston, John, 1974-
    Alyssa Milano/John Bankston.
        p. cm. — (A real-life reader biography)
    Includes index.
    ISBN 1-58415-040-8
    1. Milano, Alyssa—Juvenile literature. 2. Actors—United States—Biography—Juvenile literature. [1. Milano, Alyssa. 2. Actors and actresses. 3. Women—Biography.] I. Title. II. Series.
PN2287.M6325 B36 2000
791.45'028'092—dc21
    [B]
        00-034922

ABOUT THE AUTHOR: Born in Boston, Massachussetts, John Bankston began publishing articles in newspapers and magazines while still a teenager. Since then, he has written over two hundred articles, and contributed chapters to books such as *Crimes of Passion*, and *Death Row 2000*, which have been sold in bookstores across the world. He currently lives in Los Angeles, California, pursuing a career in the entertainment industry. He has worked as a writer for the movie *Dot-Com*, which begins filming in winter 2000, and is finishing his first young adult novel. In addition to being a writer, John is also a model and actor. He played a rioter as an extra on an episode of "Charmed" with Alyssa Milano, which first aired in May 2000.

PHOTO CREDITS: cover: Globe Photos; p. 4 © WB Network; p. 12, 13, 14 Globe Photos; p. 23, 28 © WB Network
ACKNOWLEDGMENTS: The following story has been thoroughly researched, and to the best of our knowledge, represents a true story. While every possible effort has been made to ensure accuracy, the publisher will not assume liability for damages caused by inaccuracies in the data, and makes no warranty on the accuracy of the information contained herein. This story is neither authorized nor endorsed by Alyssa Milano.

Table of Contents

4

Chapter 1
"I Can Do That!"

Many kids have watched a television show or a movie and thought, "I can do that." Many others have imagined being an actor. Sometimes children think about being famous, or having a job where they pretend to be someone else.

When kids see a play, they sometimes picture being up on stage, performing before an audience. Although nearly everyone has dreamed about what it would be like to be famous, few people get the chance.

This is the real story of a young girl who did get the chance.

Although nearly everyone has dreamed about being famous, few people get the chance.

It was early in 1980, and a little girl was watching a Broadway musical with her parents. Broadway is a neighborhood of theaters in the middle of Manhattan, in New York City. It is one of the best known theater districts in the world. Musicals like *A Chorus Line*, *Les Miserables*, and *Phantom of the Opera* have all been seen on Broadway.

In the early 1980s one of the best known and most successful musicals on Broadway was *Annie*. It was based on a popular comic strip from the 1930s, and told the story of an orphan girl's quest to find her parents.

In the audience, a girl only a few years younger than the play's star watched with fascination. The girl's name was Alyssa Milano. "I looked at my parents and said, 'I want to do that,'" Alyssa told *Maxim* magazine, "and they were like, 'Yeah, right.'"

But, in less than a year from that day, Alyssa would turn her words into reality.

Alyssa Jane Milano was born on December 19, 1972 in Brooklyn, New York. Her mother, Lin, was a fashion designer, and her father, Tom, was a music editor.

Alyssa was an only child for many years. Like many children without brothers or sisters, she was creative, independent, and related well to adults. All of these qualities would help her in her chosen career.

Because its cast included so many preteen girls, *Annie* always needed new talent. This is because as the girls got older, they outgrew their roles. Girls who wanted to be in *Annie* would perform parts of the musical for the people who cast the show. This is called an audition. There were regular auditions to replace members of the *Annie* cast. There were also auditions for the touring company. The touring company would perform *Annie* in theaters across the country.

Although she was only seven years old at the time, Alyssa Milano

Although she was only seven at the time, Alyssa convinced a family friend to take her to audition for *Annie*.

convinced a family friend to take her to an audition. She didn't tell her parents. More than 1,500 young girls tried out. Only four were picked. Alyssa was one of them.

She was too young to play *Annie*. Instead she was chosen to play July, one of the orphans. Unfortunately it wasn't for the Broadway play, which was in a theater close to her home. It was for the touring company. If she took the job, she'd have to leave home and school.

Being in a touring company means being in a different city every week. It means missing friends and family. It's difficult even for an adult, and Alyssa was just in elementary school.

Still, it was something she wanted to do very badly.

She convinced her parents to let her take the job. She left school and got a tutor—a private teacher. Although she would occasionally go back to school, she would spend most of her time away from the classroom. "Being tutored on the set was really important to me

Alyssa was chosen to play one of the orphans in the touring edition of *Annie*.

academically," Alyssa told *In Style* magazine. "I was never good in a classroom; I was an odd, creative loner child and I dealt better with adults."

Alyssa would be on the road for over a year. When she returned to New York, things were very different. For one thing, she wasn't going to be an only child for very long. Her mother gave birth to Cory—Alyssa's baby brother—in 1982.

Meanwhile Alyssa commuted regularly to Manhattan from her parents' new home in Staten Island (like Brooklyn and Manhattan, Staten Island is a borough of New York City). In Manhattan she auditioned for everything from plays to movies. Slowly she began to get more and more parts.

Alyssa played Adele in a musical version of the nineteenth-century novel *Jane Eyre*. She performed at the New York Ensemble Studio in a play called *Tender Offer*. And she acted at Manhattan's Second Stage Theater. She

She begged her parents to let her take the job.

It would take a television show to change Alyssa's life.

also got a role in a movie. In 1983 she had a small part in the film *Old Enough*.

Despite her work on the stage and in movies, neither would change her life. It would take a television show to do that. In just a few years Alyssa Milano would be one of the most famous teenage girls in the entire world.

Chapter 2
Who's the Star?

It takes quite a bit of work and luck to get a program on television. Every year hundreds of tryout shows, called pilots, are filmed. Very few of these pilots ever get on the air.

Actors who want to work in television audition for pilots. In 1983, Alyssa Milano auditioned for the pilot that would change her life. She didn't even get a chance to look at a script before her audition. She gave what is called a cold reading. That means she had to convince the people who cast the show that she could do the job, despite being unfamiliar with the show.

In 1983, Alyssa auditioned for a new TV show called "Who's the Boss?"

Alyssa was only ten years old when she got the part of Sam on the hit TV series, "Who's the Boss?"

The show for which she was reading was called "Who's the Boss?" The star was Tony Danza, a former boxer. He was best known for playing a cabdriver on the 1970s show "Taxi." On "Who's the Boss?" he would play Tony Micelli, a man who moved from Brooklyn to work as a housekeeper for a wealthy Connecticut woman.

Alyssa auditioned for the part of Sam, Tony's daughter.

Although "Who's the Boss?" was written with Tony Danza in mind, it could have been written for Alyssa. Sam was Italian-American. Alyssa was Italian-American. Sam was from Brooklyn. Alyssa was from Brooklyn.

She got the part.

"Who's the Boss?" premiered on ABC on September 20, 1984. In addition to Danza and Alyssa, the show featured

The cast of "Who's the Boss?": (left to right) Katherine Helmond, Tony Danza, Judith Light, Danny Pintauro, and Alyssa Milano.

Judith Light as Tony's boss, Katherine Helmond as Light's mother, and Danny Pintauro as Light's son.

Going from being mainly a stage performer to a TV actress would be a big adjustment for Alyssa. She'd be

Alyssa with star Tony Danza on "Who's the Boss?"

working much more. She'd be better known. But the biggest change was that she would have to move.

Although "Who's the Boss?" was supposed to take place in Connecticut and New York City, it was filmed in Los Angeles, California. When it was time to go West, her father quit his job. He and his daughter left their home and relocated to Los Angeles. Lin stayed behind with Cory so she could sell her business. A few months later she and Cory followed Alyssa and Tom to Los Angeles.

The entire family moved to California because Alyssa got a job on "Who's the Boss?" It wouldn't be the only thing that would change. For while Tom Milano began working as a music editor on films like *The Hunt for Red October*, Lin would take a different job. She would manage her daughter's career. That means she would help Alyssa make decisions about acting projects and other business decisions. Lin would also receive fifteen percent of everything Alyssa earned. It is a job Lin Milano still has.

Playing Samantha Micelli was the role of a lifetime. "Who's the Boss?" was supposed to be about Tony Danza's character, Tony. But audiences really liked Sam. Slowly the scripts featured more and more of her character. Alyssa Milano's role became like Fonzie on "Happy Days," or Alex P. Keaton on "Family Ties," in that her character went from a supporting part to a central part. Alyssa became the show's break-out star.

Chapter 3
Her Rise and Fall

Although "Who's the Boss?" made Alyssa Milano a star, it wasn't always easy for her to find other parts.

In 1985, however, Alyssa was given the role of Arnold Schwarzenegger's daughter in the movie *Commando*. That small part led to an even bigger opportunity.

Commando was shown on television in Japan. Soon Alyssa was getting piles of fan mail from overseas. An executive with a Japanese music company noticed her increasing popularity in his country. He learned she had been in musicals

In 1985, Alyssa appeared in the movie, *Commando*.

before joining the cast of "Who's the Boss?" He offered her a recording contract.

From 1989 to 1992 she recorded five albums. With titles like *Look in My Heart*, *Do You See Me*, and *The Best in the World*, these albums were never released in the United States. However, overseas each of them went platinum—meaning they each sold over one million copies.

At about the same time as she was recording music, she was involved in another project. In the 1980s adult actresses like Jane Fonda made exercise videos. Alyssa decided to do one for girls her own age. About the video, *Teen Steam*, Alyssa told *Stuff* magazine, "It was a really cheesy thing, but it was a cheesy era."

Alyssa also appeared in a number of TV movies, including *Dance 'til Dawn* and *Crash Course*.

The 1980s were very good to Alyssa Milano. For her work on "Who's the Boss?" she won three Youth in Film awards. By her mid-teens she was

She recorded five albums that were never released in the United States.

making over $500,000 a year. On her sixteenth birthday she received a BMW convertible.

Unfortunately for Alyssa, the good times would not go on forever.

Every show on television gets a rating. These numbers determine where a show ranks compared to other shows. "Who's the Boss?" had very good ratings for ABC. Throughout the 1980s the show was one of the most popular programs on the network. Girls watched the show because they liked Samantha Micelli's sense of humor and independence. Many boys watched the show because of the way she looked.

Still, as the 1990s began, "Who's the Boss?" became less and less popular. Every week the ratings went down. In 1992 it was canceled. The decision was hard on everyone.

"Whaddaya kiddin' me?" Tony Danza told *People Weekly*. "You have a kid grow up with you from the time she's ten till she's nineteen, it's pretty tough to let them go."

The good times would not go on forever.

For Alyssa the concerns were even greater. As she later told *In Style* magazine, "I wasn't really sure if I would work again." It seemed like the end of her dream.

In 1992, "Who's the Boss" was canceled.

Chapter 4
Alyssa's Comeback

Alyssa had to look for new jobs.

When "Who's the Boss?" was canceled after eight years, Alyssa Milano was almost twenty. She had spent nearly half her life as Tony Micelli's little girl. She was ready to grow up.

She started looking for new parts to play. Oddly, she followed in the footsteps of another young actress eager to grow up: Drew Barrymore. Although Barrymore was best known as Gertie in the movie *E.T.: The Extra Terrestrial*, she, too, was trying to become known as an adult actress.

In a highly-rated TV movie Barrymore played the part of a real-life troubled teen, Amy Fisher. Alyssa also played Amy Fisher in another TV movie. She starred in *Casualties of Love: The Long Island Lolita Story.*

Barrymore's first major adult movie was called *Poison Ivy.* Alyssa starred in *Poison Ivy II.*

For several years after her television show ended, Alyssa appeared in what are often known as "B" movies. These are movies which are made for very little money and usually aren't shown in movie theaters. Instead they are sold on videotape and shown overseas.

Some of these "B" movies include *Embrace of the Vampire* and *Deadly Sins.* As Alyssa later told *Stuff* magazine, "If I wanted to work, these were the roles I had to play. It took me a while to get over that hump."

While she was working in "B" movies, Alyssa also had the opportunity to produce a play. *All Night Long* was staged in Los Angeles.

She made a TV movie about Amy Fisher called *Casualties of Love: The Long Island Lolita Story.*

In June 1993 Alyssa began filming the movie _Double Dragon_. The movie was based on a popular video game. Her co-star was Scott Wolf. Although he wasn't well known then, he would go on to star on the TV show "Party of Five."

It was love at first sight.

The two dated for several months, moved in together and got engaged. Alyssa even got a tattoo of Scott Wolf's initials on her right ankle. Unfortunately, the relationship didn't last. Wedding invitations were in the mail when the pair broke up. Alyssa has since referred to it as "an awful heartbreak for me."

Following the breakup Alyssa devoted more of her time to work and less to dating. One of the films she made was called _Hugo Pool_. It was directed by the father of actor Robert Downey, Jr. Although made for very little money, it was not a "B" movie. Alyssa was proud of this movie.

Hugo Pool would give her the opportunity she needed. But the opportunity wouldn't come from the movies. The opportunity would come from television.

Hugo Pool, the story of a young woman pool cleaner in Los Angeles, attracted one famous fan. He was able to

David Charvet and Alyssa Milano from the TV series "Melrose Place."

see the movie even before it was released, and he liked what he saw. His name was Aaron Spelling.

Aaron Spelling is a television producer. That means he puts together all of the things—like actors and writers—needed to make a television show. Some of the shows he's produced include "Charlie's Angels," "Hart to Hart," "Dynasty," and "The Love Boat." In the 1990s he produced "Beverly Hills 90210," a show in which his daughter, Tori, had a lead role.

The Guinness Book of World Records lists him as the most productive producer of all time. In 1997 one of his most successful shows was "Melrose Place." Set in Los Angeles, the show dealt with the problems of a group of people in an apartment building. Starring Heather Locklear, it was one of the Fox network's highest rated shows.

When Spelling saw *Hugo Pool*, he decided to offer Alyssa Milano a part. For the second time, a television show would change Alyssa's life.

Chapter 5
A Charmed Life

When Alyssa Milano joined the cast of "Melrose Place" as Jennifer Mancini, she was nervous. The show had already been on for several years. Thomas Calabro, who played her brother on the show, told *In Style* magazine, "Everyone wonders what sort of attitude there's going to be, especially if someone's had a measure of success, but Alyssa is a doll."

For Alyssa, "Melrose Place" was different from "Who's the Boss?" On that show all the actors started together. On "Melrose Place," Alyssa felt like the new kid. As she told *In Style* magazine,

On "Melrose Place," Alyssa felt like the new kid.

"Even though I never went to one, it felt like the first day of high school. I didn't know who to sit with at lunch, so I just went into my trailer. But they were great."

Alyssa enjoyed playing a TV character so different from Samantha Micelli. On "Melrose Place" Jennifer was a schemer who went after whatever she wanted. Alyssa also liked being on a show where the women were in charge.

Being on "Melrose Place" did more to remind audiences of Alyssa's talent than any of the movies she made after "Who's the Boss?" Once again she was on magazine covers and getting the kind of attention that comes from being on a popular TV show.

Alyssa appeared on "Melrose Place" for just over a year.

Meanwhile, Aaron Spelling was planning another television show. Warner Brothers, a movie company, had just started a television network called the WB. This network mainly features shows that appeal to kids and teens.

Her character on "Melrose Place" was very different from Samantha Micelli.

Shows like "Buffy the Vampire Slayer" and "Dawson's Creek" are on the WB.

Spelling was developing a show for the WB about three sisters. These sisters were all witches who had inherited a book of spells and a house in San Francisco from their mother.

One of the sisters was played by an actress from another Spelling show, "Beverly Hills 90210." Her name was Shannen Doherty. The other sister was played by Hollie Marie Combs, who had been on the show "Picket Fences." The third sister was to be played by actress Lori Rom. When Rom had to leave the show, Spelling knew who he wanted to replace her.

Alyssa Milano joined the show "Charmed" just a short time before it began filming. Her character, Phoebe Halliwell, was the youngest sister. Both flaky and adventuresome, it was a fun character for Alyssa to play.

When the series debuted on the WB, it was the highest rated show for the

Alyssa went on to star in the TV show "Charmed" as the youngest sister.

network that week. Once again Alyssa Milano was on a popular program.

Speaking to *YM* magazine, she noted that like "Buffy the Vampire Slayer" and "Sabrina the Teenage Witch," "I think it's really cool that all of these shows have strong, independent young women who are taking control of their lives."

Alyssa (left) co-stars with Hollie Marie Combs and Shannen Doherty in "Charmed."

Another thing Alyssa enjoyed was having two other "television" sisters. Like Alyssa, neither Combs nor Doherty had real life sisters. "Since we spend about 14 hours a day together, we have completely adopted one another," Alyssa told *YM*.

In 1998 Alyssa met musician Cinjun Tate at a friend's party. Tate was the singer and guitarist for the Louisiana rock band Remy Zero.

The two dated for less than a year. They were married on New Year's Day at the Rosewood Plantation in St. Amant, Louisiana. It was a small wedding. Among the thirty guests were her co-stars, Shannen Doherty and Holly Marie Combs. Danny Pintauro, Alyssa's co-star on "Who's the Boss?" told *People Weekly*, " I hope they last a long time."

Sadly, the pair didn't. Less than a year later they were divorced.

Alyssa continues to find work in movies, including the 2000 film *Buying the Cow*, in which she plays a dancer and

Alyssa enjoys having "television sisters" as she never had any real sisters of her own.

an ex-girlfriend of the character played by Jerry O'Connell. And according to her mother and manager, Lin Milano, her daughter is hard at work on a book of poetry. The book will include poems Alyssa wrote when she was on "Who's the Boss?"

In 1999, Alyssa made progress in stopping celebrity pornography on the internet. She and her mother started Safesearching.com, which is a free search engine, where fans can type in a celebrity's name and not have to worry that scary things would come up. They also started Cyber-Tracker to protect celebrities' images on the internet.

Alyssa has had plenty of ups and downs in her life and career, but she has always enjoyed acting and has always done her best to stay in the field she loves. Her success proves that with a little good luck and lots of hard work, anyone can have a charmed life.

Though Alyssa has had many ups and downs in her life and her career, hers truly is a charmed life.

Selected Filmography

Buying the Cow (2000)
Blink-182: The Uretha Chronicles (1999)
"Charmed" TV Series (1998-present)
Hugo Pool (1997)
"Melrose Place" TV Series (1997-98)
Jimmy Zip (1996)
Deadly Sins (1995)
Poison Ivy II (1995)
Casualties of Love: The Long Island Lolita Story TV movie (1993)
Confessions of a Sorority Girl TV movie (1993)
Conflict of Interest (1993)
Double Dragon (1993)
Little Sister (1992)
The Canterville Ghost (1986)
"Who's the Boss?" TV series (1984-1992)
Old Enough (1984)
Annie Broadway musical (1980)

Chronology

Index